Round Oak School & Support Svc

PEOPLE THROUGH HISTORY

PEOPLE AT HOME

by Karen Bryant-Mole

WAYLAND

PEOPLE THROUGH HISTORY

People in the Country
People in the Town
People at Home
People at Work
People Having Fun
People On The Move

First published in 1996 by Wayland (Publishers) Ltd.,
61 Western Road, Hove BN3 1JD, England.

© Copyright 1996 BryantMole Books
Edited by Deborah Elliott
Designed and Typeset by Chrissie Sloan

British Library Cataloguing in Publication Data
Bryant-Mole, Karen
People At Home- (People Through History Series)
1. Title II. Series
643. 0941
ISBN 0 7502 1659 X

Printed and bound in Italy by G. Canale & C.S.p.A.

Contents

Cleaning	4
Washing clothes	6
Having fun	8
Keeping in touch	10
Eating	12
Playing	14
Using water	16
Cooking	18
Gardens	20
Lighting	22
Bathing	24
Moving house	26
Washing up	28
Glossary	30
Books to read	31
Index	32

Cleaning

In the past, all cleaning was done by hand. Cleaning a house used to take many hours. Nowadays, we use machines to help us clean our homes.

1900s

Few homes had electricity. Everything had to be cleaned, scrubbed or polished by hand. Rich people often had servants to do this work.

1940s

By now, most homes had electricity. Electrical equipment, like this vacuum cleaner, helped to make housework quicker and easier.

Now

Today, there are vacuum cleaners that can pick up dust and wash the carpet at the same time. Modern central heating makes much less dust than the old coal fires that used to heat most homes.

Washing clothes

In the past, all clothes were washed by hand. Nowadays, washing machines and tumble dryers do the job very quickly.

1910s

One of these women is using a washing dolly to move the clothes around in a tub of water. The other woman is wringing water out of the clothes.

1940s

Many people still used a wash tub. This tub is fitted with a mangle. The rinsed clothes were put through the mangle which squeezed out the water.

Now

Washing clothes today is much less work. We just put our dirty clothes into a washing machine, choose the wash programme and press a button.

Having fun

Years ago, people did not have the radios, CD players, televisions or video recorders that we have today. They had to make their own entertainment.

1890s

Reading, playing card games and board games or making music were the most popular forms of home entertainment.

1950s

Some people had radiograms. They could either listen to radio programmes or relax with their favourite records.

1960s

Televisions became very popular. Most people had televisions that showed the pictures in black and white. Colour televisions were very expensive.

Now

Today, many people have video recorders. People can video television programmes and watch them later. Films can be hired and played on video recorders, too.

Keeping in touch

In the past, people kept in touch by letter. Now, they can talk to friends on the other side of the world using the telephone.

1890s

This man is writing a letter. He is using ink and a quill pen made from a feather. Before people had telephones in their homes, writing was one of the few ways of keeping in touch.

1930s

Telephones made keeping in touch easier and quicker. You did not have to wait for a reply to your letter. However, even by the end of the 1930s, fewer than a quarter of all houses had a telephone.

Now

Today, almost everyone has a phone in their home. Some people have cordless phones which allow them to walk around and talk as they get on with other things.

Eating

Years ago, people ate foods which were produced locally. Nowadays, we can enjoy foods from all around the world.

1900s

This family is having tea on the lawn. Rich families could afford to eat well. They sometimes had cooks to prepare their meals. Poor people were less well fed. They ate a lot of cheaper foods such as bread and potatoes.

1940s

During the Second World War, there was less food available. Many foods, like sugar, butter and meat, were rationed.

Now

There is a wide range of foods available in the shops. It is brought here from all over the world. Many people like to eat healthy foods that are good for their bodies.

Playing

In the past, when there was a lot less traffic, children played outside in the street. They made up singing and skipping games. Today, children usually play in their own homes.

1890s

Children of all ages played in the streets around their homes. Horses with carts or carriages were the only traffic.

1930s

Although there were now cars on the roads, many children still played on the pavements in front of their houses. These children are riding their trikes.

Now

Today's roads can be very dangerous. Parents prefer their children to play in the house or in the garden. Lots of children enjoy playing computer games.

Using water

Today, we just turn on our taps and water flows through.
In the past, most people had to get their water from a well or wait for someone to deliver it in buckets.

1890s
Many houses had no running water. This man is a water carrier. He drew the water from a well and sold it for a penny a bucket.

1900s
These boys are pumping water from a village well. A metal bucket filled with water was very heavy. It was hard work carrying home enough water for a family.

1930s

Although many people had water piped into their own homes, some did not. These children are collecting water from a tap that was shared by a number of families.

Now

Today, pipes bring water into all our homes. We just turn on the tap and have water for drinking, cooking, washing or cleaning the car.

Cooking

Years ago, people cooked over an open fire. The fire was used to heat the room, too. Nowadays, most people use cookers or microwaves to cook their food.

1890s

This man is waiting for his kettle to boil. The kettle is hanging over the hot fire. The object next to it is a pot hook. Cooking pots could be hung from this.

1950s

Most people had either an electric or gas cooker. They were clean and easy to use. The heat could be turned on simply by twisting a knob or lighting a match.

Now

Many people like to use a microwave oven because it cooks food more quickly than an ordinary cooker. Microwaves can be used to defrost food from the freezer, too.

Gardens

Through the years, people have used their gardens in different ways. Some grow food there, others use gardens as play areas. Some gardens are just pretty to look at.

1910s

Many rich people lived in houses with large gardens. They paid gardeners to look after the garden and to grow their vegetables.

1940s

When food was rationed, people began to dig up their lawns and flower beds and grow vegetables. Some people kept chickens, too.

Now

Today, people in town houses often decorate their yards with hanging baskets and flower tubs. Many people have paved patios which can be used for play.

Lighting

The first lights in houses were candles and rush lights. Now, people can have as much or as little light as they want just by flicking a switch.

1890s

This room was lit by gas lamps. People had to light each lamp by hand. The gas was piped into the house and then down thin tubes to the lights.

1900s

People still carried paraffin or oil lamps around from room to room. These lamps did not give out very much light and often made rooms look dark and gloomy.

1950s

Electric lighting could be turned on at the push of a switch. Unlike today, this switch was on the end of a cable that came straight down from the light fitting.

Now

Today there are lots of different lights to choose from. Spotlights are popular in kitchens. People can even use dimmer switches to control the brightness of their lights.

Bathing

When we get dirty we can have a bath or a shower. Years ago, people had to use a jug and a bowl to wash, or fill up a bath using buckets of water.

1910s

Many people did not have baths in bathrooms but used a metal bath tub instead. In winter the bath tub could be put in front of the fire to keep the bather warm.

1950s

By this time, many people had baths in bathrooms. Some people, like the family who lived in this house, turned one of their bedrooms into a bathroom.

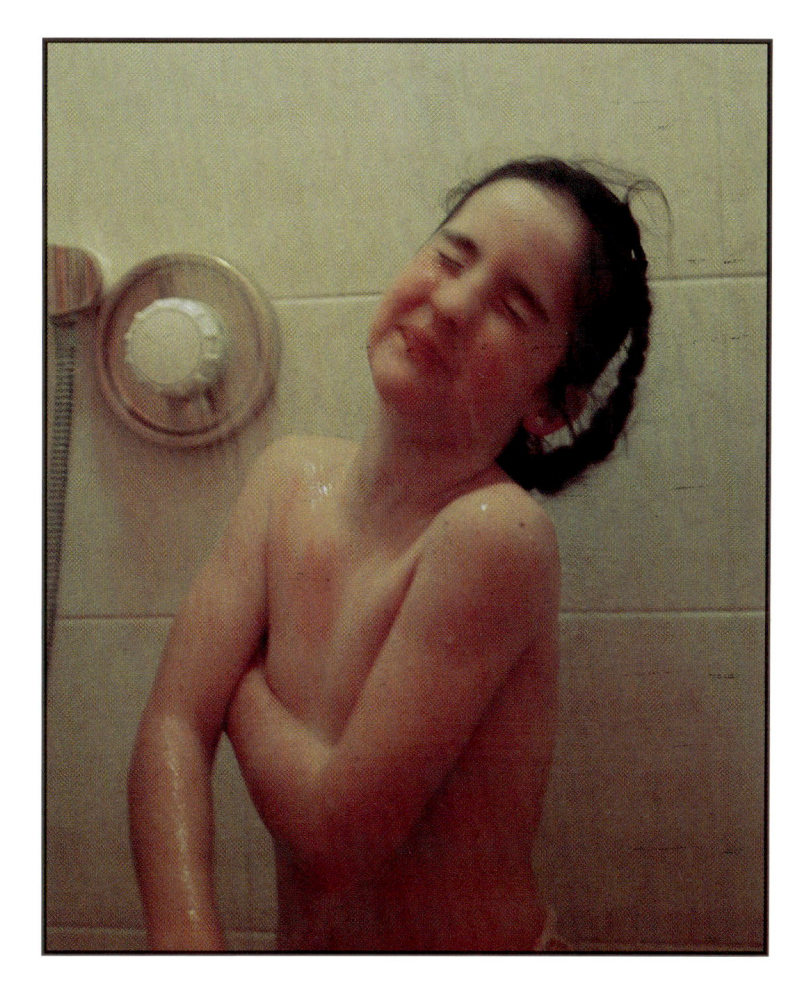

Now

Lots of people today have a shower as well as a bath. You can have the water as hot or as cool as you like.

Moving house

Years ago, most people had fewer belongings than they do today. Nowadays, when people move house, their furniture is often loaded on to huge lorries.

1890s

When this couple moved house, their belongings were piled on to a cart. The horse pulled the cart to their new home.

1940s

Relatives and friends helped this family move their belongings into their new house. Most people did not move very far away.

Now

Today, people often move to new homes a long way from their old homes. Many people use special removal companies who will pack up their belongings and take them to the new home.

27

Washing up

In the past, people had to wash up by hand, using soap and water. Today, many people use a dishwasher to do the work. The dishwasher uses hot air to dry the dishes, too.

1930s

This woman washed up in a stoneware sink. The dishes drained on a wooden drainer. She probably had to carry the hot water to the sink from a kettle or water heater.

1950s

This woman only had to turn on her tap to get hot water. The sink and drainer are made from enamelled metal. They are set into a fitted kitchen unit.

Now

Many people today have dishwashers. Everything is loaded into the dishwasher and then the machine gets on with the work.

Glossary

drainer — the tray by the sink where you put dishes that have been washed

enamel — a special paint that does not crack when it gets hot

entertainment — ways of being kept amused

paraffin — a type of oil used in lamps

rationed — when food is shared out so that everyone has a fair share

rush lights — candle-like lights made by soaking dried rush stalks in hot, melted grease

Second World War — a war fought between 1939 and 1945

washing dolly — an object that was moved around in a wash tub and helped to clean the clothes

Books to read

History From Objects series by Karen Bryant-Mole (Wayland 1994)

History From Photographs series by Kath Cox and Pat Hughes (Wayland 1995-6)

How We Used to Live 1954-1970 by Freda Kelsall (A&C Black 1987)

Looking Back series (Wayland 1991)

Acknowledgements

The Publishers would like to thank the following for allowing their pictures to be used in this book: Beamish, The North of England Open Air Museum 4, 6, 7 (left and cover), 8 (both), 10, 12, 13 (left), 14, 15 (left), 16 (both), 17 (left), 18, 19 (left), 20, 22 (both), 23 (left), 24, 26, 27 (left), 29 (left); Cephas,17 (right, David Burnett) Chapel Studios/ Zul Mukhida 5 (right), 7 (right), 9 (right), 11 (right), 13 (right), 15 (right), 23 (right and cover), 15 (right, Tim Richardson), 19 (right, John Heinrich), 21 (right, Catherine Gellatly), 25 (Debbie Bradstock); Eye Ubiquitous 27 (right, Paul Thompson); Hulton Deutsch 5 (left and cover); Positive Images 9 (left); Topham Picture Source 11, 25 (left), 28.

Index

baths 24-25

central heating 5
cleaning 4-5, 17
cooking 18-19

dishwashers 28, 29
drainers 28, 29

electricity 4, 5, 19, 23
entertainment 8-9

food 12-13

gardens 15, 20-21
gas lamps 22

kettles 18, 28

lighting 22-23

mangles 7
microwave ovens 18-19
moving house 26-27

oil lamps 22

playing games 8, 14-15

radiograms 8

showers 24, 25

sinks 28, 29

telephones 10-11
televisions 8, 9

vacuum cleaners 5
video recorders 9

washing clothes 6-7
washing dollies 6
washing machines 6, 7
washing up 28-29
wash tubs 6, 7
water 6-7, 16-17, 24-25, 28-29